KIN DRE D

KINDRED

KIRLI SAUNDERS

This is a Magabala Book

Leading Publisher of Aboriginal and Torres Strait Islander Storytellers.

Changing the World, One Story at a Time.

First published 2019, reprinted 2019, 2020 x2, 2021 x2, 2022 x2, 2025 x2
Magabala Books Aboriginal Corporation
1 Bagot Rd, Broome Western Australia 6725
www.magabala.com e: sales@magabala.com

Magabala Books is assisted by the Australian Government through Creative Australia, its principal arts investment and advisory body, and publishes with support from the WA Government.

Magabala Books is Australia's leading independent Aboriginal and Torres Strait Islander publishing house. We acknowledge the Traditional Owners of the Country on which we live and work. We recognise the unbroken connection to traditional lands, waters and cultures. Through what we publish, we honour all our Elders, peoples and stories, past, present and future.

Cover design by Jo Hunt
Cover image iSKYDANCER/Shutterstock.com
Typeset by Post Pre-press Group
Printed and bound by Griffin Press, South Australia

ISBN 978-1-925768-89-3 (print)

A catalogue record for this book is available from the National Library of Australia

*For the heartful humans that prompted these poems,
and for mother earth, who cradles us all.*

MOTHER

EARTH CHILD

LOVER

MOTHER

MATRIARCHS

~ For Mum

Here's to you
and your soul
that is drained
but carries on giving

to you
who is tired
and restless
but keeps on

to you
so close to breaking
and yet so strong
so determined
to hold it together

for someone else
for something else
for something bigger
than yourself.

DISCONNECTION

Little one,
I see you mouth empty spaces
for a mother's words to fill
and stretch your ears
for the stories and their voices.

I watch your
trembling limbs
ache to shake
in dance
and hear your lungs
as they gasp with songs unknown.

I feel your
body sans
spirit,
ceremony
and secret

and know that
it has been grown
with roots
wrenched
from the earth
that cradled them

and I taste the hunger
you do
to know the parts of yourself
to feel at home

when your
Dreaming has been taken.

MOTHER

Mother,
I've spent hours now
searching for myself
in the symmetry of your skin,
and the blues and greens of your depths.

I watch the sand dance to your tides,
and see the tannins
like tea
tessellate upon your earthy limbs.

I find my feet in the foot holes
of our old people,
long gone now

and I know
this
is where I belong.

AUNTY

~ For those that bear the scars of our past

I press my fingertips
to the scars of your forearm
and trail the stitch marks
as my eyes well,

and you tell me
that your insides
aired themselves that day.

That tissue saw sunlight
for the first time,
when a canyon
was carved into you
by someone assigned
to provide you care.

And I wondered
if it was with care
that they took you away
and settled you in a home,
away from
your flesh,
your blood,
your bone;

if it was with care,
that you were given
their brand.

UNBIND

Unbind your
seeking heart

cup it in open palms
turned to Father Sky,
as offering

to Grandfather Sun
in gratitude with grace

to Grandmother Moon
with faith

allow spirit to guide you
with timeworn map of
ancient passage,
passed down
in spoken story

and walk softly here,
for you are an ear
to our Ancestors,
and a mouth
to carry their song—

they have readied you,
guiding your path
all along.

DEAR ANCESTORS

I just want to make you proud,
to carry your stories
back to the water
they were birthed in

to show little eyes
where to look

to leave prints
for little feet
to follow

to rehome your strength,
your voice,
your spirit,
in the bodies
of future Elders

to teach them
how to listen
more than they speak,
just as you
are showing me.

TRAILBLAZER

Blaze your trail
into the valley
as calligraphic record.

Trace the shadow
of its depths
with your steps.

Navigate ravine
and gorge
and find in their folds

the springs
that form creeks

that nourish rivers

and feed the sea

learn that a journey
through darkened gully
is your start
to being free.

THIS IS IT

Allow these words
neon
and cursive
to be your sign
to take
the long way round

to finish
what you started,
to say what you mean,
to know love
in uninterrupted fullness

to read
that poem
and pen your own,
to sit
with the sun
and the moon
who sit always by you

to forgive yourself,
to forgive that hurt,
to chase that dream

to do whatever
your heart requires
to remain beating
in full force.

Let this be the sign
you've been waiting for.

OLD SPIRITS EMBODIED

Messenger birds
gather on this landing.

Spirits of the earth

that sing in
sandstone voice
and tell stories
of Mother
from a time
gone before.

Messenger birds,
that drop feathers
as echoes
of our history

of the Earth
and her creation.

Messenger birds
that share
our secrets
for those with open
hearts
and curious ears.

MY APOLOGIES

~ Written on Dharawal Country with Dharawal translations informed by Aunty Jodi Edwards

I scoop you up
in my hands
and hold you tenderly
with tear stained cheeks
as I recite a monologue
of apology
on behalf of anyone
that has ever branded you
with a name that isn't yours,

that has ever called you
earth
sand
sun
sea
salt water
escarpment
fish
moon
bird
tree.

Here,
you are
nguru
widjud widjud
wuri
gadu

pallanjang
merrigong
mara
djadjun
budjan
gundu.

NEW CHAPTER

Cut ties
and free fall
into this new book smell—

your next chapter awaits
with possibility, aplenty

in this taintless space,
you are the cultivator,
the artist,
the narrator,

with heart and
mind alight go
forth, and
create.

NOTE TO SELF

Surrender
yourself
to the process

to the dreams
that work
while you rest

to the spaces
you create
that feel empty

and to all
that is born
from your chest.

Welcome
the strangers
that love

and release
the lovers
that leave

that which is
for you
will find you

you need only
give in
and believe.

DETOUR

This is for you
taking the dirt road

for you,
veering away
from the path

for you,
who feels lost
by river bend
or cliff top.

'Off road'
will still deliver you
to your next destination

will still carry you
to where you're
supposed to be

will still move you
toward your
wildest dreams

and as you move,
so you will become
all you seek

stuck in transit,
on the road less travelled,
you are an ever-wondrous thing.

REINVENTING

This is the breaking,
the shattering,
the smattering
of every limit
ever accepted
or imposed—

the resisting,
redesigning,
the rewriting
of script
and story—

the setting,
of standard,
and boundary
and goal.

The doing
and the being

the Dreaming
and the knowing

the awareness that
this magic is yours.

This magic is yours.

EARTH CHILD

THE ARTIST

You are still here

at one now
with the earth
that beats
and breathes

with spine of fern
and skeleton of fallen leaf

with flesh of songbird
and voice of thrumming
insect wing

with touch of breeze
and stretch of sprouting seeds

with sigh of crow
and stride of sprawling trees.

You are still here.

SACRED SPACES I

I wash the grief
from my hands,
in the pool at the Men's Place

let my tears
add to glacial depth

let them shape the stone
that has held our secrets.

I am not meant to be here

am not to know of this gentlemen's place

but the Ancestors welcome me
as a daughter,
as a grandchild,
as I remember
one of theirs.

SACRED SPACES II

And so I walk

trace my toes
in the trail of mothers
gone before us

follow the wail
of good ja gah[1] ,
the joyous hymn
for new arrivals.

I sit with the Earth's
umbilical cord,
wrap myself
and reconnect,
I draw my first breath

fill my lungs
and steady my beat
for the stream

in this Women's Place,
I am tear-stained cheeks
with spirit exhausted
and body aching

I am the start
of new life

the old one abandoned
by gum tree.

1 good ja gah - baby

ELOUERA

Draw lips over my heart
it is loud about this place
where mother cradles us all
between the mountains
and the sea.

TRANSPLANT

I travel home
to press my feet to the earth
we were raised on,
to ground myself in familiarity,
to grieve you.

I pull the abundant sprouts that you'd sewn in me
like weeds,
fumble for the root of it all
and grasp at the depths
of their seeking.

With prickled skin,
I lift,
extract
and then transplant.

Carefully, I tend with the hope
that they might flourish
with transcendent flowers,
might nourish with
ripening fruit,

that they will go to seed,
and remain in the place
that we once grew,

and that one day
we might return to find a garden
alive with all that we were,
thriving
on a love that we knew.

DHARAWAL COUNTRY

Bark like hanging noose
gumnut widow maker
water, enough to drown in
there is trauma here.

Wasp nest with spider skeleton
ants, like homicide crime scene cleaners
windows barred
new trees
old scars
there is trauma here.

Wilderness fenced
cicada broaches pinned to rough flesh
bloody sap leaks secrets
there is trauma here.

Ashen limbs ache to heal
shattered sky threatens to fall
pine in place of eucalypt
there is trauma here.

RAIN

You are
the breaths
that catch
between
first
strikes
and sky songs

the torrents
of
healing
for which
Mother Earth
longs

the pricking
of skin
with
barometric

drop

the dreams
finding minds
under
rainy
roof
tops.

PLANTING

When I contemplate leaving—
uprooting from all of my promises—
I kneel in the garden
with heels to leg backs
and ears to the earth.

Here, I take counsel from camellias
and reason from the weeds
that are familiar with such things,

and as they yield ancient wisdom
from lives passed,
I listen
and dirty my hands.

I begin to water,
to cleanse,
to feed,
to plant

to tend to my chains
like daisies
that ground me here—
with the knowledge that I'll be back again tomorrow
and for all of my tomorrows,

until I grow roots
and become one of theirs.

RAINMAN

You tell me 3pm,
tilting an ear for the black cockatoos,
watching ants scatter,
sensing Father Sky
moving closer.

You tell me 3pm,
that's when she'll arrive
with thunderous announcement
with flashing lights,
you say the whole city
will rise up from their seats
to greet her,
that she'll rattle roofs
and leaf litter.

You tell me 3pm,
knowing you've been right before,
knowing you're a messenger
of our Old People
and The Earth,
and so I believe you.

You tell me 3pm,
and we wait
counting down the minutes,
temperature drops,
clouds gather.

I watch your face
instead of the clock's

I know it can't be long now.

BE STILL

Delicate soul,
make time to be still.

Lie in fields of flowers
and hear their petals hum

let their rhythm become yours
and bloom as they do,
in the places people least expect.

Know your roots
and grow from them,

climb ever to the sun
and have the shadows
fall behind you.[1]

1 After the common proverb 'Keep your face always toward the sunshine – and shadows will fall behind you'.

BETWEEN THE MOUNTAINS AND THE SEA

~ Written on Dharawal Country with Dharawal translations informed by Aunty Jodi Edwards

Rough, green, and rolling,
Merrigong is as wild as the flowers that bloom here,
banksia, wattle, flannel,
and waratah.

Trees, Dharawal warriors,
watching and protecting,

velvet valleys,
slumber on lullabies of Ancestors,
absorbing the sweet sounds that
echo between the bibara and gadu.

WIRRITJIRIBIN

~ Written on Gundungurra Country with Gundungurra translations informed by Aunty Velma Mulcahy and Aunty Trish Levett

Wirritjiribin (the lyrebird) is the most knowledgeable creature on Gundungurra Country. In the Dreaming Story of the waratah, Wirritjiribin is the one who remembers. The lyrebird is one of Kirli's personal totems.

arise wirritjiribin
tangara your truth
across the daoure
mirren ngununggula yoongaba
to the winyooa

Lyrebird – The one who Remembers

arise lyrebird
dance your truth
across the earth
sing sings of the people
to the sun

WILDFLOWER

I picked these
to remind you

that there is a place
for your struggles.

These,
the most sacred of flowers

grow only from dust
and dirt.

SEASONS PASSED

Do not take the seeds
from seasons passed
and sow them now
with the dream
that they will sprout

in a space meant for another,
in a time
a little warmer,
and with more light.

They will not grow.

They will not gleam
in dripping sun
just as you hope

but others will

with blooms bright
to ink your gaze
and fruit ripe
to fuel your days,
with roots, deep
to hold you strong
as all unfurls.

BE PRESENT

Ripple back
into this moment

inside the intermission
of expanded cartilage

between inhale
and exhale—

oxygenation
and release

stretching
and stilling

chaos
and calm

amid now
and then

the future
and the past

with gratitude
for what is.

GRIEF

They were right, it
does come in
waves, that hold you
under, as you writhe and
ache, for a surface
that you can't
place

that pull your mozzarella
body in every direction,

that swallow your breath, again
and again

and just before the Stockholm
syndrome kicks in, and
you befriend the
depths,
branding cheek with sand graze—
it wanes

and you wade
exhausted to the
shore—
where reminders
lap at your flesh
and promise that

it won't always be like this.

MT BATUR

Under full moon
with tired eyes
we followed dim lights
into the night
and up rugged mountain.

One foot
in front
of the other

we were
a steady cadence,
a simmering of souls
united in silent transit.

And when we fell
we rose,
and when we slipped
on volcanic aftermath
we stilled

and started again.

We were there
to race the sun,
to sit breathless
above golden clouds
before the dawn,
to hear her speak
her molten magic.

We were there
to rise as one.

QUAKE OF THE EARTH

She quivered
the shivers of a woman
turned cold with lack of love,
and then she shook
with wretched sobs
that moved us,

and all of the ups
came down
and the ground
was drowned in ceiling plaster
and chandeliers.

And in the aftermath
I thought of you,
and of the nights spent
between those walls
now crumbled.

And I longed for the dry season
still and
lit with new love
and for your body and mine
to collide,
like light fittings
and tiled floors,
like smoke detectors
and skirting boards,
like balconies
and bedroom doors.

I longed for us
to fall,

for us
to be more than
what stood there before.

COCOON

Go willingly
into the solitude,
into the darkness
and the light
at the end

into the space
between,
laden with breath
and limbs outstretched,
reaching new truths

hear the echo
of heartbeat
like sonar
at this unchartered depth

trace the poems
in veins and fascia
back to hands
that wrote them

bow your head
to the atoms
that utter
original ideas

shake the shadows
that followed you—

detach your doubts,

there is no longer love
for them here.

SANDCASTLES

We gasp
after the wave swallows

as tide gnaws
sand
and apprehension,
shell
and heartache—

the landscape morphs

and hands forge
kingdoms from aftermath

sculpting strength
from crumbing grit.

DOWN IN THE VALLEY

Smoke signals
pool in the
valley
trapping traipsing travellers—
in silent space
willing them
to take refuge—
to rest
to slow
beating chest
and humming mind
to mute the ego
that chatters
misdirection

to find calm
among cabbage palm
and at the base of she-oak
and gum

to stand tall and still
as they do

to be at one
with crescent moon
gloriously half-formed
finding wholeness.

BUNDANON

the messenger birds
are loud today

they persist through shouting winds
in joyous resistance

placing clues
in feathered form
along the path

they sketch trails
with crumbs
calling us
across rugged range
with sacred songs

carry on

carry on

carry on

MANDOLIN MUSINGS

It is a slow pluck
to mastery

a wind-down ritual
in breaking evening silence
with fingers
and strings
that move clumsily

forming calluses—
the unfamiliar
becoming known.

A ceremony
to mark the promise
of more melodic tomorrows.

SLEEPING BAGS AND SWAGS

Green and cream tartan
soft as smoky cheeks
and whiskey warm
this is our Friday abode.

Where we sleep
with the stars
and read to the moon

where we navigate
lost paths
to discover parts
of ourselves
in the sounds of the night
and in the morning sun.

LOVER

HEALER

Healer,
a ritual of marigold and peppermint,
with hands outstretched
that rock silk hammock
and welcome rest

with lips
that ink skin with honour
and body adorned in virtue.

Healer,
with shutter fingers
and bokeh eyes
that sculpt land
and skyline

with tender heart,
and gentle voice
of knowing

with soul songs
in a button down,
over degustation.

Healer,
a safe place for woes over wine,
with mind that is ever kind,
a spirit affixed to mine.

A DANCE OF HANDS

You and I
were the lychees
sucked
from blistered
shells,
and navel to cheek
park sleeps

the skating of
fingers over cracked palms
and the tempura
kisses awaiting
trains.

We were
the space held—
so that traumas
could surface,
speak and heal

and the rising of chest
as spine lowered
and breath slowed.

You and I,
were the footsteps through
crowded bookshops on
sacred Sundays
our tales
untold

we were
the welding of wine
to tongue
in an unnamed pub.

You and I
were handmade cakes,
window notes,
pocket poems,
and bodies coiled
to rising sun,
or the calm
of late night story.

We were time-travellers
with slow motion lips

eyes talking over
ginger tea sips

and hearts euphoric
on eurythmic beat skips.

TONIGHT

You look

an awful lot

like a poem

I'm yet to write.

MATCH TIN

Smuggled in pockets

the kindling
for conversation

between
pauper
and the upper class

between foreigner and
neighbour alike.

The crackle
of a fire
unborn

the comfort
of hands warmed
on ship deck
over unknown sea

the remnant
of a past life
of Father
and of home.

CHASING TRAINS

- For Dad

And I hope
there are still days
for wearing
soot-soaked
Sunday dresses

for hair messed
with gushing steam
from green engine

that there's time
for standing
on mountainous bridges
with the ones
you love the most

and that in those moments
you look down in wonder
at the power of

picking 'em up
and putting 'em down

picking 'em up
and putting 'em down

picking 'em up
and putting 'em down.

I hope even
when your nights
are sleepless
and your days endless

that you rise early
on the sentimental whistle
passing through the poplars—

that you always
have time
for chasing trains.

TOTEMIC LOVE

Today I want to cuddle
your naked underbelly,
to hold claws
like new-born hands
and dust sand
from peach-flesh feet

I want to smooth
spine
upon spine
as you round yourself
into the earth,
sacred
and safe

to sit by you
until you emerge
with new message,
and embark again.

THIS CITY MISSES YOU

~ For Naomi

you are
a yellow bike
kneading Glebe pathways

The Block in
tree pose (vrksasana)
and the ukulele hands
cradling
an old-fashioned
at The Eveleigh

the spots
of a dress
that belly laugh
down Spice Alley

smooth Single O on York
and the stories bubbling
from pho
at the Galleries

you are
Newtown green tea
poured for dumplings

late nights at The Enmore
and Hordern
and a 1950's cover

anytime

anywhere

ADIEU

The sky cries
as you go

heavy tears
that hang in the air
and cling to those
that venture here

pooling us as one,
a storm in a cup
neon and lagging

all lungs and limbs
holding tight

until we bid you

adieu.

SISTER

- For Pip

Mentos wrappers under couch cushions

pancakes before hockey

and little legs that always win.

The happy-go-lucky laid-back live wire with all the questions.

the sun-kissed doer

the dream chaser

the little one on plus-sized horse.

The castaway

the leader

the Golden Child.

Christmas on Leopold St,

unfinished hugs

and the one

we miss

the most.

BROTHER

~ For Jess

The eldest
the trendsetter
the adventurer

the protector
of sisters
from bigots
the powerful
and the enraged

you're the promise
of a winning billy cart
on derby day

the first lesson
in learning to write

the contagious laugh
at our dinner table

the honesty
of a heart
that beats loud

a heart
that is true

the first sought
opinion

the medium-rare roast lamb
that gathers us
that nourishes us
in times of grief

the underdog team jersey
worn proudly

and the satisfaction
of a day's hard work.

BLUR INTO BEING

Hold me again
like that,

the world stops
for us when you do,

and our beats flow as one.

Move with me here
like ink
and water,
in edgeless
unity

let us blur
into being.

MONDAY MORNING

In those binding moments
we welcome home
our higher selves
greet them
at the edge
of our being
and honour
the God
and Goddess within

we ground
ourselves
in the heavens
of the now

reconnect
recalibrate
and re-emerge

more whole
for giving

more whole
for having

and more whole
for knowing

a love
like ours.

WILLING

I sing you to me
each still night

with chords
silently spoken

to the folds
of your soul.

A melody—
magnetised
atom and ion
to pull you
in my direction

to harmonise.

EMBODIED

I have waited lifetimes
for our souls
to be embodied
in the same
form

and not as
the
flower
and the bee

the
barista
and the tea

the
arborist
and the tree.

THE LOVE YOU DON'T BELIEVE YOU HAVE

you search for the love
you don't believe
you have

in ocean
earth
and vine eyes

in peony lips
and bee sting nips

in velvety nape
like petal

in succulent flesh
more hardy
than your own
but just as needy

of warmth
and light

you turn over leaf
and stone
in the bones
of beings

to see the skin
of a river—
to find a mirror

to touch the hands
that seek blindly
like yours

for the love
they don't believe
they have

M MMMM MMM

You've got 3am bedtimes
in your cheeks

prayer eyes sealed,
in Sunday light
and Cupid's bow heavy
with words unsaid

that now arrive
like late
autumn winds
as mumbled
muffled
things

hummed like
unfamiliar hymns

M mmmm mmm

I stare at you
in disbelief

M
mmmm
mmm

You repeat—
louder

eyes still closed

M
mmmm
mmm

to make certain
I heard it
right this time,
as if this
wasn't the first
or last

M mmmm mmm mmm

I reply.

FOREVERS

Standing barefoot
and toe to toe
in nature's lounge room

you brushed my hair
from sun-stained cheek

held my hand

and promised me
with hungry lips

that you'd make
me believe
in forevers
again.

HOLD MY HAND AND RUN FAST

Hold my hand and run fast
for all we have is this moment

breathe me in as a necessity
as if without me you might drown

feel me
warm like the sun on our backs
and know

that should tomorrow bring with it our end
that I have loved you

for all you were
and all you are
and all you will ever be.

THE ONE WITH THE CAMERA

Cut out moments
so that we might hold them
once more

capture the first dance—
and the last

those uninterrupted intimacies
of beings unburdened

the seconds
that have passed—

now embalmed,
burnt
or buried—

moments that
can breathe again
for having known
your touch.

BOWER BOY

I've left blue letters
on the windowsill
for you
since I was a child.

Inked notes
on bottle caps
and pegs
and ribbons
to remind you
that we were lovers once

a lifetime ago.

My offerings for your
wild cobalt nest:

to have you know that,
Bower Boy

I love you still.

NOSTALGIA

My walk home
in spring
smells like
childhood piano lessons
dipped in jasmine
tapped out
like three note songs
elevated on telephone books

hands rounded
around black and white ivory
as if holding an egg
in palm
with fingers
counting down
the moments
until I could be done

until I could rush
to the kitchen
and hide behind sips
from a cup

until I could gush
at my first crush—
the artists' son
who I rarely
see now
or even often
think about

but who is brought
back to me
with the opening
of buds
each September.

PLAY THE BLUES

Let the gone love go,
shift capo
to 5th fret—
wrap fingers
over string
and board

look for lessons,
form blisters
on finger tips

write songs
from shards
of heart
left behind

and mend the ache
as you slide fingers
around neck
and across pearl.

STUBBORN HEART PANTOUM

I love your
stubborn heart
and its
unabashed poetry.

stubborn heart
you grow
unabashed poetry
from barren grounds.

you grow
light
from barren grounds
in these moments.

and it's
in these moments
I love your
light.

TRAIN STRANGER

You—
with pen in hand
burning the page with holes

the dirt of the day
on your soles—

are divine.

You—
with eyes alight
and dreams bright and bold—

I watch you
as you mould
the world outside.

You—
the artist
the seeker
the dreamer—

are sacred
like the sun
that bows
to mountain
on our journey home.

FIRE KEEPER

Whiskers balayaged
with stolen kisses

marks of wisdom
above the ears,
and the eyes of Father Sky
holding us all

like
          daydreams
like
          stars.

The hands of time
paused between second
and minute

and the grounding
of salt and sand
on skin.

The touch
of the fire keeper
laden with ritual

an old flame
wise   and   warm.

POPPO

- In loving memory of our Dearest Pop

Slippers too small
with the toes cut out,
black with one
in green mug,
and eyes that see
in colours more bold
than the rest.

The finger prints of
paint and pastel,
the offer
of another piece of cake,
and the M20 heart
purring with rebuilt parts.

The one with the stories,
the marker of
height and year
on fibro wall,
and the
single
word
card sign-off.

The long-way-home drive,
the green thumbs
cultivating life,
saviour
from seaweed
and from fire.

Coffee at *il locale,*
a lion badge
proud and loyal,
the classic car manual.

NEW YEARS WISH (PART I)

-For Lanie

I hope the goddess within you—
shy with self-doubt—
makes herself known
to the world
this year

that with nimble hands
she carves a stone
for your path
with every one
of your steps

that her lips curve
with yours
as you smile
at strangers.

I hope she rehomes
the ocean's gleam
in each one of your eyes

and that in her confident presence,
you know yourself

to be just as fierce

and just as healing
as the sea.

I hope that everyone else
knows this of you too,
as I always have.

NEW YEARS WISH (PART II)

- For Noo

This year
I hope a rebellion brews
in every splinter of you

and that you reclaim
every moment spent wondering

every chance never taken

every ounce of love
given but not received in return.

I hope you riot each day
to retrieve the parts of yourself
that feel amiss

that you learn not to question intuition
and that divine guidance finds you.

I hope you and your fears
finally have it out
and that peace
swells in the aftermath

that your powers
reveal themselves in the setting dust

that you see yourself just
as I do

and that to yourself
you stay true.

KINDRED

~For the loves that leave us to chase dreams.

Even with space between,
our paths still wind the same

still bend
and fold
and melt

to align our spirit
with purpose

still pull
and pool
and flow

as parallel tracks
as maps
to soul mates

still babble
and snake
and slow

allowing us to
connect
and reflect

to grow in ways
we might not have.

Even with space between
I know

that on our journeys
though diverse

we are not alone.

THE JACKPOT

The lottery ticket
I bought him
bears the scars
of wallet wear
and the tired
wrinkles of a
truck driver
with a lifetime
on the road
just arrived home.

It sits now
on the side board,
that awaits renovation—
impatient

and I remind him
again
to take it with him,
to check it,
that we may
have won.

He takes my hand,
plants roses
on my cheeks
with his kisses
and he whispers

'it's already done—
just look at this life
just look at this love'.

A REMINDER

The chance of you being
born
to your creators is
one
in
four
hundred

trillion.

You are more than
one
in
a
million

more than just
a windswept pillion

clinging to the waist of life.

LAST IMPRESSIONS

~ For the Queen of Queens

our last exchange
was an offering

we need to go for a ride

to chase the sun
at full speed
unburdened

to accelerate
down open roads

to lean in
and scrape knees—
to rock denim and leather
like second skin

we need to go for a ride

to feel the wind
lick eyelash
to move with the purr
of mechanical dreams

to paint the dirt with thunderous story
to rattle the air
so it's never again
the same—
we need to go for a ride

KINTSUGI

Read bodies
with three
finger pulse checks

count the troubles and
and trace the ripples
back to the pebbles
that started them

pinpoint pain,
trigger trauma,
and release them

still the world,
and weld
spirit with being.

Raise vibration,
and scent space
with calm

seal the eyes
and provide other
ways of seeing—

rest
the restless

and find ease
in bodies
seized

gift relief
to those in need
of healing.

YOGIS

Back flat
or
u
o n
r d
we are
the dog,
the cat
and the cow
the mind-set reset
with body
inverted
or

b
o
u
n
d

and the honour found
in daily
namaste.

The tree,
a spirit
f r ee
to flow

the strength
of a body
ho ll ow

and mind quiet
when gently s l o w e d
        in shavasana.

The balance
earned
with persistence
a yin hold
        releasing
        resistance
the mind
embracing presence
        for the
        first time

The cultivator of
      g h
    i   e
  h   r
      frequency

the body moving
        efficiently
a soul with raised
        self-efficacy
and hands
        to
        heart
        centre
with   love
        for
        all.

SELF CARE

step off the grid
        write instead

pour tea

        find melodies
that mimic heartbeats

        s t r et c h
and breathe

contemplate
        why honeysuckle always
        climbs the tree clockwise

if it is the sun
        who chases
        the moon
or vice versa

why we look
        at plant skeletons
        and see
        homes

could we see
that home
in our own
        bones?

swim, sweat
        or cry

eat something green

rinse
and repeat

rinse
and repeat

PARED BACK

And when
my hands cripple
with writer's block

and my pen seizes

when I'm
without original idea
or accolade

and my lips
are drained
of every
last
smile

when my eyes leak

with exhaustion

when my confidence
wanes, replaced
by arrogance
or self-doubt

when I am
a raging
storm

or the
feather caught
in one

when I forget
why I started

or what
I'm fighting for

will you love me still?

SANS EGO

We're tricked into thinking
we have to
have it

or do it

to be it

but we don't.

We

forget

that.

Kirli Saunders is a proud Gunai woman. She is an international children's author, poet and educator. Kirli is the Aboriginal Cultural Liaison at Red Room Poetry. She founded the *Poetry in First Languages* project. Her first children's picture book, *The Incredible Freedom Machines* (Scholastic), illustrated by Matt Ottley, is published in French and English and has been nominated for CBCA Picture Book of the Year 2019. Her forthcoming titles include *Our Dreaming* and *Happy Ever After* (Scholastic), *Afloat* (Hardie Grant) and poetry Collection, *Kindred* (Magabala). She has been recognised as Runner-up in the Nakata Brophy Prize and Highly Commended in Black&Write. Her poetry has been published by Cordite and Overland and is embedded in infrastructure at Darling Harbour and the Royal Botanical Gardens, Melbourne. Kirli has been a Writer in Residence at Bundanon Trust and The Literature Centre, Fremantle, for 'The Sound of Picture Books'.